STORIES TO GATHER

ALL THOSE LOST

STORIES TO GATHER

ALL THOSE LOST

ONA SIPORIN

PHOTOGRAPHS BY SCOTT T. SMITH

UTAH STATE UNIVERSITY PRESS

LOGAN, UTAH 1995

Library of Congress Cataloging-in-Publication Data

Siporin, Ona.
    Stories to gather all those lost / by Ona Siporin;
  photographs by Scott T. Smith.
        p. cm.
    ISBN 0-87421-185-9
    1. Siporin, Ona. 2. Siporin, Ona--Journeys. 3.
  Utah--Biography. 4. Iowa--Biography. I. Title.
  CT275.S52177A3 1995
  977.7'033'092--dc20
    [B]   94-18736
                            CIP

Cover photograph by Scott T. Smith: "Logan River at the Dugway; Logan Canyon, Utah."

Book and cover design by Mary P. Donahue
Typesetting by WolfPack

Utah State University Press
Logan, Utah

ACKNOWLEDGEMENTS

Most of these essays were first solicited as radio commentaries by KUSU-FM, Logan, Utah, and KUER-FM, Salt Lake City, Utah. I would like to thank Richard Meng, Hawk Mendenhall, and Doug Fabrizio from these stations, and the editors of *Petroglyph*, who published the first piece.

To Constance Crompton, who edited my work for KUER-FM, my particular appreciation; Constance is a fine writer and an exacting and diplomatic editor.

I owe a big thanks to Sundance Institute Playwrights Lab, where drafts of many of these essays were written. David Kranes, especially, has supported and encouraged me.

As writer/editor of the *Western Historical Quarterly*, I have been fortunate to have as employers and colleagues Clyde A. Milner II and Anne M. Butler. They have urged me to thrive, not only as an editor, but as a storyteller as well.

My friend and fellow worker, Barbara Stewart, read and typed this manuscript. She deserves praise for her gentle candor, for her technical skills, and for helping me navigate particular points of culture. Jane Reilly edited the manuscript. With a few deft changes, she made the whole of the work more cohesive, and by her attentive eye, saved me from certain embarrassment.

Michael Spooner read and believed in my work, and I thank him for carrying that trust into the reality of this book.

Finally: Steve, Dov, Lev, and Gidi.

PROLOGUE

It is 8 P.M., and I have decided to go for a walk. I will find out tomorrow that the winds tonight are 65 mph and, with the wind-chill factor, the temperature is -80 degrees. But I do not know this yet, and I think only of the walk. I dig my jacket with the coyote-fur hood out of the closet. It is an old military jacket I was given when I was a visiting poet in a prison in the Midwest. It embarrasses me to have it; every time I wear it I think of all the jackets like it and all the coyotes that were killed in order to make them: thousands of coyotes, all slaughtered for the air force. Still, I keep it. It reminds me of the young prisoners, and me, immured in the sloping stubble fields of central Iowa, all huddling in our khaki green jackets crossing the barren prison grounds to the classroom building.

When I step off the back porch, away from the protection of the garage, someone punches me in the chest. I suck air. It is the wind. I pull the hood as far forward as it will go, creating a six-inch, fur-circled tunnel around my face. It could be perfect. I am warm from the waist up and around my head, but I have forgotten to wear long underwear, and my jeans are too thin: only a minute out and my thighs hurt.

But I will not go back. I am alone with the wind, the way I want to be.

I turn left, skirt the golf course on the north, and head toward Lundstrom Park, where, on a night last summer, I lay in the grass next to the canal and watched the Perseid meteor showers. Now the park is cold and barren, the wind slapping against the ball diamond backstops. The road and walks are clogged with drifts.

Tonight the wind is in a wild dance with the snow, and the wind is the stronger partner. It howls across the surface of the streets and yards, ripping away the fine top layer of the drifts, incited to a cold stinging fog that swarms over the drifts and scuffles along a frozen gutter. Bearing the snow, the wind shifts and dodges along the ground, stops suddenly, then leaps up again, lashing my feet and legs. Across from Lundstrom, I turn west, toward the dirt hills. The wind is behind me now, plummeting down from the Wasatch Front. This wind wants me to do something wild.

I cut off the street into the dirt hills. The street is too safe, I've decided. How far do I need to go for wilderness?

Fifty yards in, the drifts are suddenly waist high and hard. It is as if I stood still and they crept in around me. I start over them, slip, regain balance just before I fall, and then slip again. I can't get a grip on the sanded snow. The drifts undulate in front of me. Sucking air, I make my way. One strong gust and I am blown down, rolling as I fall to the bottom of the drift.

Things are getting serious. This isn't suburbia, this isn't Maple Drive winding gently through one of the older developments of Logan.

A friend, Kim, once told me, "Know your place." I think of him. My place is a brick house behind a row of maple trees. Secure in that warm house, I make stew and watch the snow drift against the juniper bushes.

But tonight, only blocks away, I find another of my places. I have walked here dozens of times before, and I know now I never knew this place; I am only beginning to understand. This windtorn barren field, scarred by backhoes, disfigured by the encroachment of ranch houses, is keeping itself. The wind slaps me in the face, and I pay attention.

I push myself up to my knees, dig in the steel toes of my boots, and heave myself up, leaning hard into the wind. My hands ache, my thighs sting.

I begin to run; I am only on the edge of being frightened. Mostly, I am cold. I run in a jerky, uneven motion. My boots grip one step and slip the next, one step slides and the next sinks, waist deep. I stumble, fall, groping my way toward the road, head into a wind too painful to breathe.

My friend's mother died in a drift at the end of her street. She wanted to die there. She planned it that way, and she went there on purpose to freeze to death. She was only yards from a house.

This story I'm telling is small. It is just one of many of a season when I learned to let the snow take me. To let it gather me in with all those lost.

I.

I cannot remember if my
mother woke my brothers and sisters and me from sleep, or if
she let us stay awake until it was time. I only remember being
on the dirt road, surrounded by women in print dresses and
men in overalls and heavy work shoes, walking toward the
house that was our destination. There was no full moon; it was
dark and cool, and I could skim through this silent crowd and
the night air like a fish. Even though the shadows crossed our
way, I was safe, surrounded by my own people.

Later, I learned that we had a gentle tradition of

chivaree. Elsewhere, I heard, the men sometimes stole the bride away and hid her for days. Instead, we gathered in the lane of one of our farms, shaking hands, stifling our laughs, passing the babies from arm to arm to keep them quiet, and whispering, "Have you got a pan and a spoon?" We carried these pans and spoons, fittings from our milk separators, junk metal, toilet paper, and soap.

I could feel the dirt against my feet as we walked and the thick presence of the men and women around me. On the night air, the warm odor of these people mingled with the sweet smell of timothy hay, and the rich, golden scent of field corn, ripening. My joy was thick; I could hold it in my hand, I could walk through it. It was in my muscles, and it made me want to run.

When we reached the house of the newly married couple, who had gone on their honeymoon and come home again to begin their life, we spread out through the yard below their bedroom—Didn't each of us know every house as if it were our own?—and at the signal, we exploded, banging pots and pans, calling out "Come down! Come down!" My brothers and sisters and I ran from window to window soaping them with XXs. We toilet-papered the outhouse and the bushes at the porch. We yelled, "Candy! Candy!" titillated not only because we were being naughty, but because the adults were too; our whole community was out, in the dark, banging pots and yelling for treats. We ran wild, knowing it was what we were supposed to do. We were free in a way we were never free on other days—all because someone had been married.

Within minutes a light came on in the bedroom. We banged louder, "Treats! Treats!" Behind the house, the neighbor boy grabbed me and kissed me, then ran off laughing. I ran too, exhilarated by the kiss and the air. At the door, the newlyweds appeared, disheveled, their robes tied tightly around them, arms extended with boxes of candy and cigars. "Come in! Come in!" Their voices crackled with sleep. "You did it. You fooled us. We thought you would come last night. We went away and stayed out late."

The men smoked their cigars; even my father, who never smoked, puffed at one—and then coughed, and laughed for coughing. It was Tuesday, a week night. We ate one candy bar and then another. It was midnight. We snitched a cigar and ran behind the house. Someone had matches, and we lit up. The smoke made my head reel. I thought I would vomit, but none of it mattered. I had only to turn and plunge into the night air that covered my head and shoulders and arms and belly and legs, that flowed over my skin like a river flowing at night over rock. To move in that air was all I had to do to be perfect; I was certain of who and where I was, among people I loved, who loved me, fed me, who allowed me freedom and laughter in the darkness that, I know now, never goes away.

One September Monday, when I was a freshman in high school, I smeared egg in my hair, dressed in long underwear, and, groveling on all fours, nudged a marble down the main street of Maxwell, Iowa, with my nose.

This was freshman initiation. In our high school of one hundred students, it happened every year: the seniors were masters of the freshman for one day in the fall. Each freshman came to classes dressed as her senior had ordered, carrying a paddle and a bucket of candy. Whenever one of us encountered her master in the hall or outside a classroom, she kneeled down, and offered candy and extravagant compliments. If the senior approved, he sent her on her way, with her hair screaming at the ceiling, stiff with egg whites, and her unlaced clodhoppers banging against the wood floors.

At the end of the school day, we were paraded down Main Street, flanked by the masters, while the townspeople pointed and laughed.

The other side of this humiliation was the ecstasy of belonging. We dreaded looking foolish in front of the whole town, but we knew that by the next day, we would be new, older, and, wonderfully, members of that junior high dream: High School.

The year I was initiated, I liked everything but the marble business. My neck muscles ached, I scraped my nose, my senior repeatedly tapped me on the rear end, "Yer fallin' behind, hurry up." Before I had gone five yards, I stood up and said, "It's enough," and the senior understood I meant it.

The day passed, and I had a good time that year. The next year, a girl named K. was handed a marble and commanded to perform the same feat. She acquiesced, pushing the marble a whole block before her master relented. When she rose, her nose and cheeks were bleeding, and even her father the pharmacist could find no medicine to relieve the staph infection that distended and mottled her face for the next year.

Initiation was discontinued, of course. It's too bad. It was an elaborate tradition, a symbolic enactment everyone enjoyed: the townspeople laughed at our dress and by their laughter singled us out as special. We were the ones crossing the boundary into the almost-adult world of high school. Our junior high play clothes were on the closet floor, and the next day for sure it would be skirts, sweaters, and slacks.

When we memorized the laudatory poems and knelt to deliver them to our masters, and carried their books, these acts signified bowing to the authority of learning, study, and experience. All of us—some with parents who had never gone to high school—should acknowledge where we were, what was about to happen.

The problem was the marble. It wasn't part of the tradition. The senior who thought it up missed the point because he wanted to humiliate instead of to humble me. He wanted me to do what he wouldn't do himself—and that is not the way of initiation. K. paid for it physically, and all the kids since have paid for it culturally.

Since I left high school I have seen initiation ceremonies in Asia, Africa, Europe, and the Middle East. Each time, I was reminded of the way we created our community in central Iowa, of the way we welcomed a new stage in life, and said goodbye to an old one. In those other places, I always remembered home—and that darned marble.

My father always drank tea from a china cup. Though his hands were brown and gnarled, thick from hard work, and rough as a gunny sack, he held the cup delicately by the handle, between his thumb and first finger and slurped the tea, the way the other Swedes did. I have organized my memory of him so that what rises to consciousness are not only images like this, but his spontaneous laughter, his profound wisdom, and his meticulous sensitivity to the welfare of our animals.

But maybe it is better not to romanticize, not to

polish up history. The fact is, we kept a baseball bat in the corner behind our porch door, though none of us played ball. I did not understand what this bat signified until my thirteenth year.

That spring, we bought a breeding bull that we put to pasture in the small meadow south of the barn. Adjacent to that meadow we kept the cows, and between the two meadows, spanning the fence, my oldest brother had installed a water pump. We had run pipe from the milkhouse in a trench, under the pasture to feed the pump. It was a good fifty yards downhill, under the lot, so everyday my father checked the pump to make sure the trough was filled with fresh, clear water.

After we bought the bull, this minor chore of checking the pump became a nuisance. My father was accustomed to climbing over the barbed-wire fence, walking across the field, looking at the pump and the water, and walking back the same way, up the hill to the house. For the first few days we had the bull, there was no problem. But, after a week or so, the bull would wait until my father had reached the unprotected center of the field and then charge.

My father was a good runner. He had won the 440-yard dash and was on the winning team of the 440 relays at the Drake Relays in 1921, but age, overalls, and brogans had slowed him down. Still, he made the fence every time, but after another week, his patience was depleted.

It happened on a Wednesday afternoon. My mother and I were in the kitchen when he came through the back door. He spoke to my mother, who was standing at the stove.

"Blondie, where's the ball bat?"

My mother looked surprised. "Why, it's behind the door, right where it's always been."

He reached around and took it and walked out, gripping the bat in his right hand. I saw him pass the window. His jaw was set; he looked like the school janitor, B. J., had looked just before he slugged J. S. in the mouth for messing with his equipment. I ran out of the kitchen to follow him, but kept my distance.

The way he was moving, I thought he might walk right through the lot gate, but instead he climbed up and over it. Usually, he unlatched it and walked through; I was glad to be behind him.

I watched him disappear down the hill, and ran up to the gate myself and climbed up on top. He was at the base of the lot, squeezing the strands of the barbed-wire fence together so he could step over into the small pasture. The bull, like a dark shadow, was grazing in the corner of the field.

My father did not look at the bull, and the bull did not raise its head. As my father walked resolutely toward the pump, the bull kept grazing. I knew my father's muscles were taut; I could tell by the way he held his shoulders, and I knew the bull was fully aware of my father, so it was not a surprise when it lifted its head.

With a sudden snort, it charged. In the same instant, my father turned, spread his feet for balance, and, holding the bat in both hands, raised it above his head.

The bull galloped toward him, spittle curling in the breeze out of its mouth and nostrils. It was in a full run by the time it reached my father, and its head was lowered.

In one perfect, graceful motion, my father struck, square between the eyes and, in the same instant, jumped into the air and back, out of the way of the black carcass, which was propelled forward and down by its own mass.

For a few seconds, all motion and sound stopped, as if a movie had been frozen on one frame. My father stared down at the animal. I knew his heart was pounding, but it didn't show from where I sat. He stood perfectly still.

Then, his shoulders went limp. He held the bat, but loosely, as if it might fall from his hand at any minute; and I heard him curse, "Damn it. I killed the bull."

Though I knew why he was cursing—it was our only breeding bull, the only one, in fact, in the neighborhood—I was shocked and scared and yet, I laughed; though I believe now it was a hysterical laugh that was closer to tears than to humor. I had seen animals killed before, but I had never seen him do it, except for chickens for our Sunday afternoon dinners, and I had never heard him swear. He seemed at that moment to be someone I didn't know. The air was thick with his anger and power. I wanted to get down and run away from what I had seen, but I couldn't stop watching, because he was my father, and maybe too because in the middle of the anger and power there was foolishness: he had killed his only breeding bull. I was laughing for all these reasons.

When he turned and started toward the house, looking back once, as if he expected the bull to jump up and come after him, I jumped down and ran. I figured I better give him distance, so I ran back to my mother.

A few minutes later he came into the house, still holding the bat. He looked at my mother without saying anything, then turned and put the bat back in its place behind the door.

"Would you like some tea?" she asked him. He nodded. I watched him drink, to see if his hands were shaking. They weren't.

"I killed the bull." He said it without looking at her, when he was about half finished with his cup of tea. She didn't answer. She looked down at her hands, resting in her apron. Her head was bowed, and I bent down to see her face, but I couldn't see it, and I couldn't tell for sure what she was thinking.

They were both quiet a few minutes, and then my

father said, "I'd better go check to see if the dead wagon can get down in there. We'll probably have to tear out part of the fence."

I followed him out again, as far as the gate, to see what he would do. Just as he bent over the bull's carcass, there was a snort, and a yell, and both of them jumped up and back. The bull turned tail and ran, and my father stood his ground, slapping both knees with his hands and laughing, with an edge that sounded like crying. "Oh, the dickens! The dickens!" he repeated. I was happy to hear him say that, because that was the kind of language I was used to, and the bull was alive and had learned its lesson, and the gentle man that I knew to be my father had come back—the laughter had come back.

I don't remember the stuffing or the pie that I ate for the Thanksgivings while I was growing up in central Iowa. But I do remember the stories.

They began around dessert and continued through coffee and the cold walks along the lanes bordering the stubble fields. We had many stories.

One we often told was about the day we had to shoot our draft horses. I remember stepping into the stall with them, their powerful bodies overcome by pneumonia. Our neighbor had borrowed them to plow, but he was a flighty, distracted man and forgot to cool them down when he had finished. Now it was too late. I watched as they struggled, driven by instinct, to rise. Too weak, they could only bang their heads against the manger. It was a sickening rhythm; in my memory the sound of it filled the barn and the whole outside. They were beating themselves to death.

My father sent Joe and me out of the barn and he stood by while the vet put them down. It was the only time I ever saw my father give over this painful sort of responsibility.

Workhorses were special in a way unlike other animals. It has to do with the intimacy of the work relationship. A pet dog isn't the same—that's entertainment or pure companionship—though a sheep dog might be the same. But a workhorse the family knows and depends upon, and the horse senses it. I can't call it anything but love: I had crawled under the bellies of our horses when I was a small child, and I rode on their backs while my father plowed, or planted. I petted them, hugged them, I mussed their manes, rubbed their noses, helped my father with the traces, handled their reins, rode the planter behind them as they pulled. I helped curry and feed them, and reveled in the moist warm scent released from the manger as they ate. And all the time, I knew they were smarter than me. If they needed help to survive, we did too: it was a perfect reciprocity.

Joe and I stood on the hill. We flinched with the first

and then the second shot. Neither of us cried then. It is only since I have been an adult that I have cried.

We never used horses again. We went on to a little Ford tractor and a John Deere. By the time we were young adults, my father advised us, "Don't go into farming." It was a wise, but painful reality: he knew we would be owned by the bank and the government. One tractor could easily cost $50,000. When my father spoke these words, he may as well have said, "Let go of your past," because that is what we had to do. We five became a banker, a dentist, a factory worker and part-time farmer, a professor, and a storyteller.

I tried to go back into our farm house after my father died and my mother had moved to a home. The house is not empty; my nephew lives there, just one hundred yards from my brother's house. I stood on the porch and looked at the familiar doors and windows. I had helped repaint the house twice myself, and my father had done much of the carpentry. Turning, I looked out at our land, and then at the barn. I could hear the shots again and see Dick and Maggie swinging into the gaping maw of the dead wagon. I left.

The house was the center of our life—and without my mother and father, without the garden behind it and the horses and the milk cows in the barn nearby, it was lost. It was the place all the stories of the days and years gathered; from its porch you could smell timothy hay, manure, sweat, a fourteen year old's first perfume, the blood of slaughtered animals, the rich loam of Iowa topsoil. And now for me it was lost, now it was wherever the stories were.

Besides the story about our horses, we told about the day one early summer when Clarence was mowing hay in the field at the far end of the lane behind his house. He was on the little Ford sweeping downhill in the late morning sun toward the ditch, when he noticed a clump of alfalfa stuck on the last teeth of the mower.

Clarence was big—his waist was wide and round and he had a stiff leg, "a hitch-in-his-git along" we called it, from the time a hay door fell on him. The doctors had removed the socket and soldered his knee joint.

When he slipped the tractor out of gear and stepped off, he forgot to flip on the brake. Why? Did the warm, fragrant morning make him forgetful? Or the sight of the rolling hills thick with bushes and green distract him? Or was it the single-minded drive to solve the problem and get on with the job that urged him to his own disaster? Iowa farmers are like this; they forget to button their shirt sleeves and they wear ragged coats, so when corn-picking comes and they are too intent on the job or too rushed by the cold, they jump down to clean the snarl of stalks out of the picker and their flapping sleeves or their ragged cuffs catch and the picker pulls them in.

It is a litany: Gene pulled off his own arm to save himself; Dwayne lost his fingers; Paul was not strong enough to fight the machine, and we buried him on a bleak November day.

And now it was summer and Clarence forgot the brake, and the moment he stepped down, the motion of his bulk upset the inertia of the tractor and it slowly began to roll. It knocked Clarence off his feet, onto his back into a dip in the earth, with his left leg pointing to heaven. As the tractor rolled, that mower sang a song: *Sh-sht, sh-sht, sh-sht, sh-sht* toward him and over him, cutting off his leg just above the knee. Desperate to save himself, Clarence beetled around in the hay and the dirt to maneuver his head downhill so he wouldn't bleed to death.

Then he waited, watching the blood bubble up on the exclamation of his stump, listening to the *sh-sht* of the mower droning on at the bottom of the incline where the tractor had halted against the edge of the ditch.

My brother Jerry found him, and the surgeon at the hospital told Jerry, "It was a good mower, I couldn't have done better myself." He cleaned the stump and pulled what skin there was over the raw end, and before long, Clarence came home to work the cutting.

All the stories weren't sad. We laughed at the memory of Hick racing up the road, his car full of kids, flames shooting from under the hood—and how my father ran to the road to stop him, and he only rolled down his window to yell back: "Can't stop to talk now, Hap, gotta get these kids home before the car blows up."

We told about Joe, who went away to the army and freefell from the training plane to catch the jumper ahead of him. The man was wigwagging earthward strapped to a *mae west*—a malfunctioning chute with the lines running over the top, creating two quivering mounds of silk too woozy to carry a man safely down. We told how Joe caught him, and how they floated to earth, clasped in each other's arms.

And we told stories about a local woman of leisure who once added two zeros to a check for twenty-five dollars and got away with it because Mr. D. didn't have the courage to own up in court to visiting her.

In truth, I must remember what I ate those holidays at home; I always make the same Thanksgiving meal as my sisters and my mother. But my mind doesn't linger on the recipes. Instead I remember the house. I imagine myself inside, ranging the hallways, listening at every door. When I come to the room where I hear people laughing, crying, and recounting their histories together, I go in and sit down, to tell stories and to celebrate the gathering of my mother, my father, my brothers and sisters, my grandparents, and great grandparents, my children, and my grandchildren yet unborn.

When I was five and my older
brother, Jerry, was going someplace, I would run to him, calling: "Budsy! Budsy! Where are you going?"

"I'm goin crazy, you wanta come along?" He'd say.

"No." I would protest. "I want to go to the real place."

At the same time this exchange delighted me, it frightened me. I didn't want to go crazy. Was he *really* going crazy?

I was thirteen years younger than him; I idolized him,
and I would have believed anything he said. He was the one
who kept a bull snake asleep under his t-shirt, and when he

went into the navy, he saw a man burn to death in the waters of Lake Erie. I would have believed anything he said.

My father once ordered a set of drinking glasses that, though they were glass, were guaranteed not to break. When they came in the mail, my sister Mary set them on the big oak table in the kitchen, opened the box, and, with delight, began dropping them, one by one, on the floor. We all joined in; dropping these glass glasses on the floor, exclaiming each time, "It didn't break! It didn't break!" How I loved her in that moment—her courage, her excitement to start it all; I wanted to be exactly like her.

Mary stopped dropping the glasses only long enough to call Kenton, her future husband. "Come down and see this, Kent. They can't break." When he walked in the door, she was waiting, glass poised in hand between her thumb and middle finger. When she was sure his eyes were on her, she dropped it, and the glass hit the floor and shattered into a thousand glistening pieces. I ran under the table, until I heard Mary's—and then the others'—laughter, the laughter that in our house seemed capable of healing any break.

My sister Dana didn't know that I used to sneak into her room to look at pictures of James Dean in her movie magazines. I used to look at her manicure set too, and dream about having such slender, beautiful, and capable hands as she had. She was such a good artist that my parents had arranged for her to have lessons at the Des Moines Art Center on Saturdays, plus, she was tall enough to detassle corn in the summer and sometimes worked with the tough girls from the Mitchellville Training School. "There are things," she said to me once, "I can't tell you."

There was no way I could ever hope to be like my older brothers and sisters. These anecdotes don't touch a hundredth of the mystery, excitement, laughter, and courage I saw—and still see—in all of them. But I don't expect these stories to make sense to anyone else in the way they make sense to me. There are stories within the stories: my brother's comment turned to irony when mental illness *did* enter my life; my sister's shattered glass turned metaphor for the broken sides of all joyous moments; and James Dean—the object of my extreme and distant passion—lives on in passions that have long since replaced him. These small anecdotes are stories within the stories: the glass is broken but the laughter rings in the air of our kitchen and I hear it over the span of many years; the one who goes crazy comes back from that distant land for all the moments before she walks out on her own journey once again; and the passion for James Dean becomes the passion for a living man. But whether they are my stories or yours, they are the pebbles that shine in the darkness to lead us home.

When we went back to Iowa to visit my family, my brother gave my son two light sticks. A light stick is a plastic tube that glows if you bend it hard in the middle; jumpers use them to make patterns when they leap from the plane.

Since Vietnam, Joe has been a compulsive skyjumper. I stand in the wide strip of grass between corn fields, near Cedar Rapids, and watch him and the pilot circling in the small plane. They peak at ten thousand feet, and the pilot cuts the engine. I see Joe hurtle himself into the atmosphere. Once

I rode up in the plane with him and watched him as he moved out onto the bar, waved to me, and stepped into nothingness. I do not want to see him do that again. He smiled, but it was not a smile I understood.

I watched him and the others, jump after jump. Each time as he plummeted toward the yellow target that was home base, he waited a few more seconds to pull the rip cord. I know; I was timing him.

At seven, the pilot said he couldn't fly anymore. There was a strange noise in the plane's engine. Joe and two of the other jumpers went with the pilot to listen, but none of them could tell what was wrong. They came back, shaking their heads, the wide legs of their black jump suits flapping in the wind. None of them wanted to stop, but the pilot couldn't fly. There was nothing to do but go home.

In the van, Joe took the light sticks from the glove compartment and dropped them in Lev's lap. He didn't say anything.

We brought them back to Utah with us. The neighborhood kids used one for a game of hide-and-seek in our back yard, and we saved one. We kept it in the freezer so it wouldn't lose its power. It got shuffled behind the ice cube trays and the chickens, and we forgot about it. Then, on a hot night in August, when Lev was rummaging through the freezer looking for ice cream, he rediscovered it and ran out into the back yard, calling me to come play catch with him.

It was a clear night. Logan is at 4700 feet, and I could see the dippers and Orion. We moved to the back of the yard away from the kitchen lights, and Lev tossed the stick to me. I missed the catch. The light stick bounced across the dry grass, neon green, toward the pine tree. I stumbled and fell before I reached it, so I rolled my way over to it and scooped it up in my hands. Lev laughed.

With the stick in my hand, I stood up, stretched my arms out and twirled round. It made a living circle in the dark.

I tossed it to Lev. He took it in his outstretched palm, twirled in wild circles as I had done, and then, suddenly, stopped and threw it straight up in the air.

Against the night, in the hands of my son, the light stick had become a bridge, a narrow path spanning the dark distance between earth and stars, and at that moment it seemed to be meant not for my son and me, but for my brother, so that he could get back, finally, from Vietnam. When it fell, we ran to catch it, and without speaking we threw it up again and again, to keep it there until Joe could find it and cross home on the light that was his in the first place.

I called my mother last week to ask her how she was doing. She said, "Well, I'm not buying any green bananas."

My mother is ninety. In 1922, she was offered a job as a columnist on a big midwestern newspaper, but she left after a few days to go home to help her mother—who was lying-in with the baby that was to become my uncle.

From then on, my mother's choices were for family: she married my father, she cared for both my grandmothers during the years they were bedridden and finally, dying; she bore the five of us children; and with few exceptions, she spent her days on our farm—*Avel Mai'im*, which we understood to mean "meadow of waters."

Behind these visible choices, my mother made another choice obscured for me, until lately, by my memories of her as a mother—instead of as a woman.

I understood one day when she was in her eighties. She came wide-eyed and startled out of the bathroom. "Ona!" she blurted out, "I just looked in the mirror and you know what? I've got wrinkles. I'm getting old." She gazed at me, incredulous.

I looked at her standing there, with her bright eyes shining; her the child now and me the adult, and I realized she had experienced some kind of epiphany—like the first woman must have felt when summer ended and she saw the leaves begin to turn color and fall, and she knew a big change was coming, one a lot stronger than her.

She had known about her wrinkles for a long time, of course. They had been, like they are for all of us, a simple cosmetic fact; she had simply patted on the cream and gone to bed. But now, she looked like she had entered a foreign country for the first time, like everything about her was new and she wasn't sure she could understand or make herself understood. I could read it in her eyes: "Well, what now?"

This moment lasted only an instant between us. She

didn't change her behavior; she went on like she always had; she watched for opportunities to help, and helped; she listened much and spoke little; she loved and respected my father, and after he died, she revered his memory with a dignity that cast no shadow on the passion with which she had loved him. In the early mornings, she rose, again and again, to sit by the south windows of our house, to look out over the land that she had named, to gather her love and to will goodness in the world. It was as if in those early hours, in a living room, on a farm in central Iowa, she made a conscious choice to prevail.

When I was flown back from the Peace Corps paralyzed with meningitis, she came to sit by me in the dreary hospital room to say, "When you are better, you can help Jerry cut the cottonwood if you like." I knew then I would rise and be healthy again. When my first marriage failed and I had catapulted into another relationship, she and my father came to visit, when it would have been easy to chastise. It was not just for me: my brother in Vietnam, my sister's pure loyalty desecrated by a drunken husband; my other sister, only seventeen, alone with a child and husband, learning young to prevail on her own; divorces, deaths. . . . My mother rose and rose again, determined to glean a sensual beauty and laughter from our 160 acres.

If it was my father who told story after story and taught us by that the way of people, it was my mother—who seldom, unlike the other farm wives, worked out of doors—who taught me how to look at the land. If my father spoke, she was the silence where the words would ring. When she turned her head, our eyes followed.

Once, as a young wife, my mother was attacked by a farrowing sow while she was gardening. The sow knocked her over, then loomed above her, its foul spittle dripping from its snout onto her face. It had stepped on her arm, snapping the bone at the wrist. Later, I asked her if she had feared for her life.

"No. It's just . . ." She hesitated, as if she were embarrassed. "It's just that it had such bad breath."

This is an Iowa story that I have told you. This is what I can tell you about the courage and spirit of a woman that grew up topsy in a small town called Collins.

When I am driving up the dugway toward the canyon I think that if I get going fast enough I can fly upward to where my father will go when his cancer finds the kindness to release him. It seems to be a place over the mountains, in the air above the canyon; and I think that if I get there first and am waiting for him, then he will pass over more easily.

Since I first discovered he was dying, I have been doing this: fusing my memories of him with the mountains, the canyons, the rivers, the desert where I live. I let my eyes play tricks on me. I stare at the Wasatch Front until I see my father walking over the pure black Iowa bottomland where I grew up, and I watch as he reaches down to take and study a handful of the rich earth. My father could observe the crows and know when it would rain, and he could cure gall by putting a rock in his pocket. When we were sick, he chased us through the house balancing a hot toddy in his hand. "Drink. It will make you well," he called, as we scattered before him like starlings. *He* never took a drink in his life, but he knew the medicinal qualities. In his gentle spirit, he kept one field virgin in tribute to the earth and the grasses. During the months he was dying, I ached for this language of our farm, the knowledge that I shared with my first family—the sounds that I had stopped speaking when I left home.

This obsession to feel near, to communicate with my father in the last months of his life, began last winter, when Steve and I were out on a walk by the reservoir, what we call First Dam. I looked across toward the ice-shelf that had formed on the far side and spread toward the middle, and could see two critters hunkered on the edge of the ice, feeding. At first I thought they were beavers, but it was ten o'clock in the morning, and we were walking along a traveled road, I couldn't believe that beavers would show themselves.

The next day, I went back to the reservoir with

binoculars. They were muskrats, and they were there still, huddling in pairs, gorging themselves.

I watched. One slipped off the ice into the water and disappeared. In a few minutes it resurfaced with a fresh load of vegetation from the bottom of the reservoir, struggled up onto the ice, and turned again to its frantic feast.

I began going everyday, sometimes two or three times, and I included Second and Third Dams in my rounds. At Third Dam, up the canyon, there were seven, eight, even nine of them feeding at once. I identified their mounds in the shallow waters of the marsh behind the dam.

It got so all I wanted was to watch the muskrats. I made up excuses to leave work early; then, I would call the babysitter to tell her I had to work late. I lied to my children. In the afternoon, when the older ones came home from school, I told them I had errands to do and that they would have to watch the baby. They moaned; I got in the car and headed up canyon.

Once, on my way to Third Dam to watch the muskrats, I spotted a bald eagle perched on the branch of a log that was wedged in the cattails of the upper marsh. I swung off on the side road and eased out of my seat, leaving the door ajar so I wouldn't scare it. Crouched down, I moved along the bank downstream. Just as I approached the bridge that spans the neck of the marsh, the eagle dipped into the water, grasped a fish in its talons, and rose into the air, flying downstream faster than I could ever follow. I watched it disappear around a bend. I thought it lifted above the ridge again to light in a barren aspen, but maybe I was mistaken.

Walking on toward the ice that jutted out into this wide marshy spot, I counted seven muskrats, one alone and the others in pairs, feeding. Their mound beetled up out of the water about twenty yards away. It looked as if it had been thrown together, rather than built, but I knew it was more intricate than I could perceive from where I stood. Inside it was sure to have two or three dens and a supply room.

The muskrats' shiny, chestnut-brown fur glinted in the winter sun and their short, thick heads bobbed up and down as they tore at the vegetation they had piled beside them. When one dropped into the marsh, I tried to envision its swim fringe, the bristles on the edges of the toes of its back feet, fanning out in the water, and the skin fold in its inner ear clamping down. I tried to imagine it in the liquid dark, under the ice, tearing at the vegetation with its powerful incisors. I thought of the eagle lifting into the air, farther than I could see, and this common little critter, diving below surfaces where I could never go.

And I thought of my father disappearing into What?

The element of death was one I could not imagine—surely it was not water or air.

We owned 160 acres of pure black Iowa bottomland, bounded by Indian Creek, which we dignified by referring to as the "river." While I was in school, beavers built up a dam on the creek and flooded our soybean fields. My father didn't want to kill them, so he and my older brother spent long hours destroying the dam, tearing it apart, limb by limb. Within two days, the beaver had rebuilt it. My father was patient, but the beaver were more patient. Distraught, he called the fish and game commission, and they trapped the beaver out. That would have been the end of it, except that the next winter they were back again.

He loved to tell the story. He delighted in the determination he saw in the beavers; and I know there were times when he stood under the cottonwood in his heavy shoes and bib overalls on the bank of Indian Creek and watched them rebuild their dam, while the water poured over our precious fields.

Another time I drove up river, I had the kids with me. As we turned to cross the bridge over the marsh, my middle son grabbed at me and pointed to a small, bare aspen on the bank. Perched in the top was what looked like a pygmy owl, staring at us. We stopped and got out. The owl turned to look out at the marsh; we could see the dark, wide, distinguishing slashes across the back of its head. We were not more than ten feet away and six feet below the branch where it was perched, and I couldn't figure out why it didn't fly, or why it was there in the early morning, next to the road.

Once, riding on the tractor with my father, I was perplexed to see him stop, put on the brake, and step down. We were plowing and there was no reason, that I could see, to stop. He crouched down and crept to the front of the tractor, where he bent over, out of sight. When he stood up, he was holding a bull snake, one hand behind the head, the other at the tail. Sinking into the freshly plowed earth with each step, he carried it carefully to the edge of the field and set it loose in the grass. Another day he might have carried it up to the granary, for a mouser, but he didn't need this one, so he let it go.

Another time, in the spring when he had been plowing all day, he came in at dusk and I heard him call out to my mother. "Blondie, oh, Blondie," he was calling. (My mother's hair had been black; this was some term of affection between them that I never understood.) She met him under the big Dutch Elm in our front yard. He was so excited, he was speaking to her even as he came up the little hill to the yard. "I just saw seven deer at the edge of the field, in the shadows of that big stand of cottonwood on the west side, by the dike."

I write my father about the things I see: the muskrats, the pygmy owl, the eagle, the deer that wander down our street after a snowfall. My mother tells me he loves these letters, and he asks her to ask me, each week when I call, if I have seen any more muskrat or deer, and he says for her to tell me that these are things the boys will never forget.

After my mother's last call, I sat looking out the windows at the Wasatch Front. I could see myself strolling through a newly planted field with my father. Neither of us spoke. The dream continued: I see him harnessing our work horses and feel his strong hands grasp me securely under the arms and swing me into the air, onto Maggie's broad back where I will ride while he plows. I see him throwing bales from the ground up onto the hay rack. The sleeves of his blue workshirt are rolled to the elbows and sweat is dripping off his fine, high forehead.

When my son slams the side door, it startles me from my dream: in front of me are not cornfields and cottonwood, but the mountains of Utah and, at the base of the Chinese Elm, a shafted flicker, a Utah bird, is prodding the earth for worms.

For a moment I am confused. My father, the blue-eyed Swede, has disappeared, and I wonder where I am. Then I see Lev's face appear in the doorway and my father's smile takes life on my lips. "Lev," I call to him. He comes to me at the table, and I point out the window, guiding him to the sight of the shafted flicker, to what is sacred in the world.

II.

I can sit at my kitchen table
and see gullies, scrub oak, and in the right season, mule deer
on the Wasatch Front. High up, pine speckle the hills, pacific
willow border the river; bunchgrass and sage stud the dry
rocky slopes.

For a while, I lived on the Turkistan Plain of northern
Afghanistan, in a city called Mazar-i-Sharif. It had the same
feel as Logan of being close to the mountains, but it was not
close enough to the foothills of the Hindu Kush to see such
detail as I see now.

I think often of Afghanistan, particularly in the evening, gazing across the valley to the Wellsville Mountains on the other side. It's at that time of day that I remember the dust-choked summer streets of Mazar, the cold winter classrooms of the *dabirestan* where the students and I would huddle around the *boxari* and study verb tenses, and the Hazara shepherd high in a springtime meadow, twirling in an ecstatic dance with his shepherd's staff, while the sheep grazed on the stinted hillside.

I remember my friends: Hasan, Aminullah, Rooshan, Amina. . . . I have not seen them in twenty years, and have not heard from them in ten. I wonder where they are, if they are still living. Two million Afghans have been killed. That's one-seventh of the population. Five million are in exile. Three million are internal refugees. Families have been decimated or worse, sometimes losing half to the army, half to the *mojaheddin*. Of which group are my friends?

The Soviets invaded on the twenty-seventh of December 1979. It has been so many years ago and the people so long inured to war, that the carpet weavers of Herat have added Soviet tanks to their traditional design of the tree of life.

I am not claiming a particular grief by telling you this. But because I ate with the people of Mazar, laughed with the women in the *hammam*, was stoned and feasted, had friends, and fell in love there, I sense the tanks running over ground I know, visualize the faces of the Russian soldiers—children themselves and perhaps even the sons of those Russians I met in the bazaar—as they kill and are being killed by the liquid-eyed children I taught. In Balkh, where I picked up coins from the time of Alexander the Great, sat in the tea house and ate kabobs, or rode my friend's fine Afghan horse through the back streets to the countryside, charred stumps are all that remain of the almond trees.

The things that remain for me, that I can hold in my hand, now rest on a shelf, out of context and unintelligible to anyone in our household but me: Aminullah's silver pitcher—how did he afford it on twenty-eight dollars a month, with eight people to support? How does he care for his family now? The dress that Amina made for me hangs in my closet—where is she, with her generous hands? I wear *Kuchi* earrings and walk with their gentle tinkle—where is the woman who gave them to me, who knew how to elicit their true grace, motion and sound?

What I cannot hold, lives by my telling: Hasan's generous laugh when I choose the wrong Dari word and yelled "Shit! Shit!" instead of "Go! Go!" at a horse race. The last kiss of a love I was never to see again. The ring of a camel bell in the desert dark; the terrible encounter with a mastiff high in the foothills; a magic people, whose generosity conjured food and lodging out of a bare adobe room; the threat of death from a Pushtun who guessed that American capitalism could be as devastating in the long run to the Afghan cultures as the Russian's invasion would prove; and the stoning that in memory I can cherish, though on that summer day on a narrow street behind the mosque of Mazar, I was terrified—only to be saved by some spirit of my father that spoke to me, "Well, pick up a few rocks and throw them back at them!"

In 1217, a city in Bamiyan was renamed *Shahr-i-Gholghola*—"City of Noise," for the shrieks of the dying after the invasion of Genghis Kahn. Now the Russian army has outdone Genghis Kahn. So here are my shreds of memory, finally, my only weapon.

Our neighbor, Ray, and other
friends, Helen and Miiko, bring us vegetables from their gardens: tomatoes, potatoes, cucumbers, lettuce, cabbage, beets, herbs. I always thank them, but thanks is never enough. There is more to the story.

For every event there is something happening behind it. A history. This is the part you can't thank someone for: the memory elicited, the resonance that an act carries. In my case, it has to do with cucumbers, illness, and a long trip across a foreign land.

I was in Jalalabad, Afghanistan, one of the cities of Alexander the Great, a city that, until it was senselessly bombed during the war with Russia, was beautiful, filled with ancient treasures. It was a vacation spot for Afghans from Kabul, Mazar-i-Sharif, Herat—the colder, northern cities.

I was riding a bus to Pakistan, to vacation in Swat and Hunza, and I was sick with flu. I could not eat the rice at the lorry stops. I knew the lamb's fat used to cook it would make me worse, and I could not drink, because I had no resistance to the amoeba in the water.

We had been riding for hours, sweltering in the sun and gritty with the dust blown across the Jalalabad plain, and I felt alone and helpless. The other passengers were kind to me, but what I wanted was to be back in my home in Mazar-i-Sharif, hundreds of miles north, across the Hindu Kush.

We were making a quick stop in the food bazaar and then would head down the pass toward Peshawar. I had resigned myself to discomfort and leaned my head against the window, closing my eyes, imagining the cool shade of the pergola in my own courtyard. When a ten-year-old Pushtu girl tapped against the window, I lifted my head. She was another of many beautiful Afghan children, helping her family by selling vegetables in the market. She smiled at me and held up a cucumber.

I looked at her: her face was dark, her eyes lucid. She

was dressed in a red dress and printed *tomban* (very full pants), and wore a long green scarf over her head and shoulders. Though I had not thought of it—I felt too ill to even think— I realized as soon as I saw her that she was offering a vegetable moist as a drink, one from which I could peel the amoeba infested skin. But how had *she* known?

She pushed it through the opened window. I held up a coin. She waved her hand, as if to brush the money away. Then she laughed and ran off, her long braids bouncing against her back.

There is nothing else to tell. Years ago, when Afghanistan was still a country at peace and I lived there, and I was ill, a child gave me a fresh, succulent cucumber. Why? Had someone on the bus suggested it to her, paid for it even? Was it a joke I didn't understand?

Now I live in Cache Valley, a different desert, and I sometimes discover a sack full of produce on my doorstep. When this happens, I know that my friends have done it again; they have brought me not only food, but magic: With their gifts the moment expands, I can defy time. I pick up the sack and put my face in it, to smell the rich earth and the sweet odor of fresh cucumbers. Fast as memory, I am back in Afghanistan, eating that girl's offering, forever healed by another's generosity.

Before the Russian invasion, I lived in Mazar-i-Sharif, Afghanistan. One spring day I got a phone call from the Ministry of Health asking me to fly down to Kabul and be part of an inspection team at the insane asylum.

"But I teach English as a second language!" I thought he had mistaken me for someone else.

"It's OK," the man from the ministry said, "We need somebody objective."

I took the Ariana flight south over the Hindu Kush

and caught a taxi to the asylum. The other members of the team, all Afghan, had gathered at the guard station, and we stepped through the gate into the wide, open compound that was flanked by adobe huts.

All of the insane were housed in that same compound: the men and the women, the children; the criminals and the harmless. A nude man streaked by us; in one room there was, unexplainably, a hydrocephalic child in a crib. Yet, there was no confusion. It was as if this group of people had walked away from the stringent behavior code of Islamic society and had formed a community of their own, where everyone was welcome and there were no veils.

We approached a group of women chatting around a fire. Our guide switched from Dari to English and whispered, "Notice the tall woman. When we leave don't turn your back on her."

The women greeted us, and offered us rice from the pot steaming over the fire. The tall woman stood up and came to shake our hands. She was about 6' 5", or so it seemed to me, weighed an easy 200 muscular pounds, and she embraced me with the warmth a mother might hold a child. We talked for a while, mostly to the tall one, and when we left she shook our hands again and smiled as we backed away down the hill.

"She's killed six people," the guide whispered, "all when they had their backs turned."

I like being warned like that. It reminded me of the helper figure in fairy tales, the one who always has a gift or advice for the hero: "Here, take this ball and follow it wherever it goes." Or, "Take this little box for your kindness." Or "When you come to the stables, choose the spavined nag, not the white stallion." Or, "When you approach the tall one, don't turn your back."

There were no funds for any fancy care, no psychiatrists, no medications, just this folktale kind of reality: no one, including the woman herself, could change the fact that she could become a witch—but everyone knew she was one.

Back in the U. S. a few years later, I wished I had had a similar warning when I was pregnant with my first child. The problem was simple: a cervix too weak to hold the weight of the baby. My doctor had every instrument and technique at his educated fingertips, but thought pregnant women should not be examined.

Where was my helper? Where was the one to remind me I had entered the country of medicine and things were not as they seemed? The birds help Cinderella. The trees come to the aid of the kind sister. Ivan Tsaravitch is saved by the advice of an old man he meets in the forest. My Afghan co-worker warned me away from the witch. But where was *my* helper in technological America?

My son is twenty now. He's at the university, is an

athlete, and works at night. On his birthdays I tell him the story of his traumatic premature birth and of the months that followed when he was contending with death. I also tell him the old story of Rapunzel and how, in the tower, she learns the witches' tricks, by the aid of the objects in her prison. I tell him this and other fairy tales, so he will have some basis in reality and will learn not to turn his back.

Venice begins to get warm in March. There are days when you can see a man leaning against the south side of a building, sleeping with his face tilted to the sun. Days like that the water can blind you, and the wind ruffles the canal.

On the day of *So e Zo i Ponti*, the sun sparkled on the lagoon toward San Giorgio, the water was dotted with sailboats and *sandolos*, and the 23,000 runners and walkers waiting for the race were crowding forward, jostling for positions at the front. Officials yelled through their megaphones: "Stand back! Stand back! This is not the starting line."

Massimo took me by the hand and pulled me through the crowd forward. "She's a great American runner!" he was yelling. "She will finish first! Move aside! Move aside!" I held my arms up in a pose of victory, while Massimo lied through his teeth. Five minutes before race time, the runners stampeded, surging ahead in a wild rush of cheers and baby cries and laughter. The officials scurried to the side, shaking their heads.

I looked around me. On one side was a group of school children, carrying a banner. In front of them was a team of men dressed in short skirts, sombreros, and tennis shoes. An alpine club raced with ice axes and ruck sacks; a woman guided fifty children, shouting to the crowd that they were all her own. There were a few German, Swiss, Americans, and one woman from Russia.

The race was non-competitive, but I was schooled by the Oregon Track Club and so, sprinted over the first bridge, on Riva Schiavone, trying to position myself in the lead. With a seriousness that seems laughable to me now, I burst along the lagoon, past the carnival set up for tourists, past the maritime museum, towards Giardini.

At the six kilometer mark, we funneled into a passage-way suited for two abreast. Front to back, pushed one against the other, we shuffled and shoved along the narrow walls. I spotted an old couple, trapped in a doorway, trying desperately to move out, against the flow. Exasperated, the woman began to yell, "*Basta! Basta!*" and to beat the runners' heads and shoulders with her umbrella. The runners laughed—and then too the old woman and her husband broke into grins.

Romance at the half-way point. A young Venetian fell into stride with me. We nodded at each other and smiled. He saw a break in the pack signaling me to follow. I followed. He checked to make sure I was still there; we smiled at each other and picked up the pace, aided by the adrenaline of the eyes.

At ten kilometers, after forty-seven bridges, my legs were cramped and I wished *I* had an umbrella for the crowd. Still, a breeze was sweeping in off the lagoon across the *Fondamenta delle Zattere*, and we were on the home stretch. The spectators had lined the *fondamenta* and they were cheering wildly. At the end, a large sign was stretched across the campo: *RISTORA* (rest station). Seeing the sign a group of teenagers broke into a sprint, pushing and shoving to get to the station. The campo was barricaded except for two narrow funnels. I was determined to pass through, to wait for water until the end of the race, but I couldn't. A woman behind a long table reached out and grabbed me as I skimmed by. "Eat! Drink something!" She shouted, shoving a brioche and a paper cup filled with wine into my hand.

It was one of those moments when a person enters, by

surprise, another reality. Still running, I looked at the brioche and wine in my hands. When I turned to look back, to see if I could see the woman who had given them to me, I saw a goat trotting along with the other runners.

I did run in this race. And at nine kilometers, two kilometers before the finish, a woman did hand me wine and brioche. I have a medal to show that I finished in good standing. But I think maybe all this happened many years ago, when things like that could happen.

They found Mirko's body near Rialto. I imagine Pino running, careening, breathless, along the narrow cobblestone alleys of Venice, reeling across bridge after bridge to get to this boy-man, his brother, one more time. It was too late.

The script of Pino's letter was crushed, twisted. Those broken symbols spoke before the words themselves; each time I unfold the letter to read again, the signs of grief startle me, and my heart pounds, preparing for the loss I already know.

For Pino, Vanna, Anna, Gianni, Steve, Dov and me

there was a year in that city of bridges, with the sunlight glinting on the marshes, when Mirko was courting his life, a year when he worked to reclaim his strength—after Pino had saved him from the opium dens of Central Asia and a filthy jail in Karachi. We lived with him that year. He was a young, handsome, dark Venetian with luminous, sad eyes, and he was struggling. He played tenderly with Dov, four then, and ate macrobiotic foods. He laughed until the sound of it rang off the marble floors of the small apartment we shared. But if I turned to look at him, I saw that what seemed like joy came from the awareness of an incongruous occasion, and was actually a roar, a shriek transposed for those of us around him. It was the bellow of a primitive who knew no safety or peace, who knew that this hunt or the next, he would prove too weak.

In Beadwell's *Origin of the Kiss*, there is a man who passed over a lark on the road. He glanced into the rearview mirror to see if he had killed it. It was perched, stone still, in the middle of the pavement. The man got out of his car and walked back to check. The lark, unhurt, was balanced in suspended animation, in a cataleptic spell from the shock. Not knowing what to do, in desperation, the man threw it into the air, back to its own element.

When the man threw the lark into the air, the spell broke. With its weight leaning on open sky, the bird revived and flew to freedom.

I wanted the same for Mirko, and not long before I left Venice, I kissed him. There seemed to be no other medicine but this to ease the pain and fear that soaked his eyes. I can still feel his smooth skin on my own, can still smell the moist, warm scent of his neck, can still recall the urgent need to turn him from his desperate course by some small act of love—that basic portion of us all, in which I have believed.

But Mirko had forgotten the feel of air—and I was not a princess in this real-life reversal of Sleeping Beauty.

Tonight I will rise at 3 A.M. to watch the Perseid meteor showers. As on many nights, I will sit on a hillside of the Wasatch Front and let the world settle around me—full of its light and its darkness, full of beauty and pain and memory: full of stories—the only means to gather all those lost.

We foreigners in Portugal sometimes get together. We are a mixed population of expatriates, people in business, lonely spouses of intermarriages, scholars, and people displaced by terrorism or fleeing from war in some former Portuguese colony.

One night ten of us—all women in our 40s and 50s—gathered at *Morgados* for a surprise birthday party.

Morgados is a fancy restaurant under the bleachers at the bull ring. In keeping with the ambiance, we were all dressed to kill. Ruth, whose birthday it was, wore a tight red skirt split to her perfectly formed Royal Ballet thigh.

Most of the women belonged to the same New Age study group. So, while we ate, we talked about reincarnation, signs, horoscopes. Carol figured out that I am a buffalo. Dorothy is a snake; Maureen a rat. We mapped out each other's families, and cooed when the 20-year-old son of one of the women stopped by to say hello. Each of us made a toast to Ruth.

The women were all spirited, good humored, *and* interesting. Three owned a booming real estate business together, one was vice-president of a cosmetics firm, another a clothing designer.

English and Portuguese flowed back and forth. We laughed and drank thick red wine. The Londoners sang: "Maybe it's because I'm a Londoner . . ." And then one of them embarrassed us Americans with her detailed, dead-pan description of a drive-in funeral parlor in Los Angeles.

About eleven, Ginny told a dirty joke about a princess and a frog. Then, with red-faced enthusiasm, suggested we go to the bar *Coconuts* to watch the male strippers. Ginny said the week before a woman there had pulled off one of the stripper's tongas, squirted him with whipping cream, and then licked it off.

We glanced at each other around the table, with the dirty joke and the story of the whipping cream, we seemed to have become a sad imitation of a stag party and all of us knew it. There was silence before the laughter, and then the laughter was too loud. It was as if we had wanted an intimacy together, a camaraderie—but, like little girls, had taken someone else's advice on how to do it, and had failed.

Suddenly everyone was saying goodnight. Chairs scraped the wooden floor, we snatched up our purses and shawls, and waving and kissing each other goodbye, hurried out to our taxis, our lovers, our children, our jobs. We rushed away into the darkness of the Estoril coast, searching for our own dialect.

I have just had a permanent.
It's one of those frizzy jobs that makes my hair stick out. I'm not the type to have my hair permed, but since I came to Portugal, I like spending time at the hairdressers, and a simple haircut doesn't keep me there long enough.

Portuguese hair salons have a certain *je ne sais quoi*. To begin with Patrick, (Pah-treek), who owns the shop, speaks six languages, fluently. One day I heard him give a haircut in English, discuss a color job in French, do a trim in Italian, and settle some business in Portuguese. During my perm he conversed with a woman in Dutch and while my curls were being rinsed, he chatted on the phone in German.

Fernando, with four languages, is almost his boss's linguistic equal. He rounds out the menu with Spanish.

Try to imagine this hairdo *à la polyglot*. Two French women exclaiming over a fashion magazine, rattling their gold neck chains as they speak. A British matron sitting straight in her elevated chair wearing English tweed and sensible shoes. A dark-eyed *Italiana* with deep red lips, having a sleek geometric cut. A Portuguese teenager in meticulous black with alabaster skin and perfect grace—even with a towel on her head. And me—an American—in jeans and running shoes. The only one not talking.

Or eating.

Yes. Next door to the salon is a coffee shop—or shall I say, a *pastelaria*. Mid-afternoon Fernando comes to each of us, "A Senhora, would you like coffee? Something to eat? A pastry perhaps?"

They all say yes. Fernando goes out and within minutes he comes back carrying a tray loaded with coffee cups, pastries, cheese sandwiches, and mineral water.

"Who pays for this?" I wonder. "Who cares?" I answer myself.

The woman getting the color job eats the cheese. The French women drink the espresso. The British woman has coffee with milk and the pastries.

This seems to me to be paradise. A dark handsome man has just washed my hair, massaging my scalp until I feel like jelly. I am wearing a salon smock, which amounts to a pajama top; I am warm. Everyone is kind and gracious, and now, on top of it all, Fernando is asking to feed me.

Wouldn't you want to spend time here? Wouldn't you get a perm, whether you liked it or not? *Não acha que é optimo*?

And if you want to know what that means, ask my hairdresser. He's the only one who knows for sure.

When my son and I went to Torres Vedras we met a tire salesman. He was a handsome, slight man with dark hair and deep blue eyes. He was wearing a skin-colored lace bra, tight black shorts, black hose with a hole in the thigh, and a bright red earring. We discussed the profit margin in tire sales. He asked if we were from Boston and when I said, "No, Utah," his eyes widened and he exclaimed, "Oh! Utah Jazz!"

The town of Torres Vedras has little to recommend it to tourists. The wine is good—but wine is good everywhere in

Portugal. There is the ruin of one of the Duke of Wellington's fortresses—but it's only an unimpressive stone wall. What Torres Vedras does have is a public celebration of *Carneval*. It is the only city in Portugal in which people give themselves up to three days of music, dancing, masks and costumes, street theatre, drinking, and dousing each other with water. Torres Vedras celebrates its Mardi Gras in the old Roman fashion— where everything is permitted. Everything is proper.

The tire salesman was having a difficult time moving his lips.

"How long have you been drinking?" I asked him.

"Tree days," he answered, pleased with himself.

Just then a wave of pigeons burst over us. He looked up, raised his open palm to them and exclaimed softly, "Oh, Plums."

Then he turned to me with a sheepish grin, "Plums?"

I shook my head. "Pigeons."

The street was beginning to hum. Vendors were hawking water guns, plastic masks, cellophane wigs, nuts, and fried pastries. Workmen had boarded-off the main streets leading onto the square, and the scouts were selling tickets to the parade. There was a group of men dressed as women sitting on the curb drinking beer. One had two milk cartons hung round his neck, another was pushing a baby carriage that I later learned held not a baby, but a giant phallus that popped up mischievously.

"I shouldn't sit by you," the tire salesman lamented. I am too drunk."

I took his arm, "No. No you're not."

"I'll tell you something." He leaned close to me and I knew he was about to give me an important message, "I carry two photos in my wallet: one of my mother and one of Miles Davis." I looked into his beautiful dark eyes and felt a rush of intimacy.

In the next instant, I heard a commotion and saw that the parade had begun. Junior high kids were throwing bags of ashes at the crowd from off the floats. People in the crowd were throwing them back. Men were dodging through the onlookers bopping people on the head with rubber hammers. The drummers leading the giant-headed puppets were pounding out an unrelenting rhythm, and all of us were throwing and dodging water balloons.

I've vowed to go back to Torres Vedras soon. I want to find the tire salesman and give him a Miles Davis tape. When I imagine myself doing this, I envision a sudden light in his eyes, a flicker of recognition, the small delight of an enigma, and around us, an exultation of plums.

After living in Portugal for
several months, I have decided that the American idiom "Hey!
Call me. We'll do lunch!" is a misapplication of that sturdy,
working-class verb.

Is it *doing* something to lift five bites of pasta salad to
your mouth? Or to heft to your lips a four-inch California
gourmet pizza sprinkled with duck sausage?

I've done lunch many times in the U.S. and have
never even begun to sweat. In Portugal one, simply, lunches.

The last time I lunched it was at *Eduardo's*, down by the train station. It cost $9.

First Course:

Thick, chewy bread served with a variety of cheeses and pure butter.

Second Course:

Veal cutlets smothered in mushrooms and a delicate sauce. A mountain of perfectly browned fries. A heap of tender, aromatic rice and a full liter of red wine.

Third Course:

Green salad.

Fourth Course:

Chocolate mousse.

And finally, coffee so strong you get only two tablespoons.

I know what you're thinking: They must be a people thick about the knees—it's not true. Strong, lean faces. Flat stomachs, slender arms, perfectly shaped calves. Half bikinis at the beach. Women, as they say here, "as thin as a thread of olive oil."

How can it be? One eats slowly and one walks. Lunch hour is from noon to 3 P.M. The food is savored. Maybe the calories are lulled to sleep.

But I think the main reason the Portuguese can eat

lunches like I ate at *Eduardo's* and not be overweight is that walking is a common and much loved transportation. Housewives shop everyday. They scurry to the food store and trudge home again, balanced on the return by two or four heavy sacks of wine, detergent, greens, and bread. Men walk to the pharmacy with their 80-year-old mothers shuffling along beside them. Children clamor down the street on their way to school. Teenagers stroll to the post office to pick up packages.

For pleasure, the *promenade* is the sweet sister of a leisurely meal. Sunday afternoons the two-mile walkway along the ocean is overwhelmed with locals, dressed to the teeth, admiring the sea and sizing-up their neighbor's new high heels or sports coat.

They say that time in another culture enlivens one's own culture. It's true. I have learned how to "do lunch" properly.

I'm just hoping my boss understands that it takes three hours.

When I went to Tomar for
Hanukkah I visited the castle, of course. It's what the town is
famous for, and it is an impressive monster of Romanesque,
Manueline, and Renaissance architecture. Its chapel is so big,
and the Knights Templar who lived there were so ardent, that
they attended mass on horseback. But what I really went to
Tomar to see was a synagogue no bigger than a living room.
Weaving through the tangle of streets along the river, I was
thinking about the Crusades, and about Hanukkah. Hanukkah actually means "dedication." The holiday comes from

ancient Israel, when the Maccabee family led a successful revolt against the occupying Greeks. Once they had retaken the temple, my ancestors cleaned it and rededicated the lights that symbolize the presence of G-d among us.

With this jumble of military campaigns on my mind, I finally found the synagogue. The door was open, and I stepped into the sanctuary of stark white walls and plain vaults. Senhor Vasco, the caretaker, closed his book, smiled at me, and said "Shalom."

In that instant, in what I can only, ironically, describe as an epiphany, I understood that by being there in the synagogue, I was involved in a victory of magnitude, won without swords.

The synagogue was built in 1438. Before its plaster was dry—in historical terms—King Manuel followed the example of the rulers of Spain and expelled or forcibly converted all the Portuguese Jews. Trapped in the broad palm of the Catholic Church, there was no possibility of an armed revolt this time. The Jews sailed away or lived as Catholics; and the small synagogue of Tomar was defiled.

This October, 496 years after Manuel's edict, his descendants attended the rededication of the synagogue. The building had been used as a prison, a church, a hayloft, and a grocery warehouse, but people like Senhor Vasco never forgot what it really was.

We live in a human world and will always have wars. Still, standing in the synagogue of Tomar, it was clear to me that those of us left alive can reject despair, and memory can prevail—even when other empires fall.

III.

When we were in Jerusalem,
my son, Dov, said he would lead us to the Old City by way of
Jaffa Gate. So he and his two brothers walked ahead, Dov in
the middle flanked by Lev on the left and Gidi frisking along
on the right, craning his neck to watch his older brothers talk.

I remember this particular moment because it was my
first time in Jerusalem, and because my husband and I and our
children had gathered from distant places to be together, and
because in that moment we were all happy and well.

I watched the three children walk ahead of us, in lively

relief against the wall of the Old City. Their gestures, their voices, their forms, and the shapes of the city and the passersby were clear and beautiful.

There are not many of these moments, not because they don't present themselves, but because we usually don't recognize them, and even at that moment when I did and was walking forward, I could feel myself fading, like a runner who has handed off the baton and is watching the others pull away.

The First One

On their birthdays, I tell each one the story of his birth. Dov's is the most dramatic. My water broke two and one-half months early. The doctor checked me, patted me on the arm, and leaned down to whisper in my ear, "It's OK. You'll have other children." I can still feel his breath hot on my face, can still feel his resignation trying to worm its way into my skin and taint my blood. "No." I said. "I'm having *this* child."

Did I sense then that before Dov was eighteen he would be a black belt in karate, that his friends would come to me in turn to express their thanks for his being, and that in my own worst sickness, he would come to me and say simply, "You have been a good mother for us, the best" and would embrace me—the broken one—and by his love would help me heal.

I put the doctor out of my mind. I went home and lay down for two weeks, while our friend Pino and I played an Italian card game called *scopa* and chatted in a mix of English and Italian. Then, on an early morning, I went into labor and stepped across the boundary into motherhood.

They told me to expect the worst. After twenty-one hours, I bore Dov, and before I could lift my head, they had taken him away. They wrapped me in a warm blanket and had started with me back to the room, when the young nurse pushing me asked, "Would you like to swing by and see him?" I nodded my head.

The corridor was dark, so as she wheeled me along on the gurney, my pupils must have expanded, and when we reached the nursery window, the light startled me, it was so bright. Dov was lying in a tangle of tubes in some complex sort of incubator. His chest was pumping up and down, and he seemed to me to be a bird, flailing, frantic for the right slant of air.

I broke. Only minutes old, birth had brought him this.

The nurse shoved the gurney back into the darkness. "Oh, I shouldn't have brought you. I shouldn't have brought you." As if, in saying these words, she could erase from my mind the vision of my child's struggle. She thought to protect me; but if she had not taken me there, I would have gone anyway.

Now I see him in front of me, a man, leading me to Jerusalem. I am not certain I have earned the way, but by his and his brothers' light, I am going.

The Second One

Lev was born in a prison in the Midwest. I was working as an artist-in-residence, and my family and I were given a whole cell block in which to live. We had a five-room shotgun apartment with a toilet in each room. Three flights down the back stairs, we had an institutional kitchen with a sixteen-burner stove and four ovens. My husband, who was working on his dissertation then, took this kitchen seriously: "Eat, Ona, eat." Every week the doctor's eyes opened wider. I went from 100 pounds to 150, and Steve insisted I was more beautiful than I had ever been. At nine months, with a cold April wind blowing against me, he took a side shot of me and now, fifteen years later, he still takes it out to show people. "Doesn't Ona look beautiful here!"

Lev was born with an angel's kiss across his forehead that even now shows up when he's ill or upset. When I see him flying off a ramp on his roller blades, taking in six feet of air, or watch him fling himself into the river from the high rock cliffs at First Dam, I call on that angel's kiss.

This attitude of his about life must be because at nine months old, joyous of his teeth, he bit my breast so hard I bled, and even in my pain, I laughed because he was delighted. I should have taken him off my breast, put him down, and walked out with a firm "No!" But I didn't. Now he doesn't know how to be afraid.

If you want to know this child, you have to stand in the canyon late at night and let the wind rush over you and listen to what it says.

The Third One

I became like Sarah. This was the child of my age—it started in laughter, and I am still stunned by the joy. His birth story was so common, it delights only us. Especially, he likes to hear how big he was at birth, and that I ate a steak dinner after, with roses in a vase on the table. He is only six, but plays the piano with a concentration that I have only dreamed of, and when we lived in Portugal, he learned to speak a fluent Portuguese in what seemed like minutes. I hold his face in my hands and look in his eyes and try to read what will happen, but I am not allowed to know the futures of my sons, only to discover, from a certain distance, a part of what will come.

Notes About Being A Mother

There are children that are, and children that are lost. One way to know about a woman with children is to know first, as an African woman told: that she is a mother; that she is and has always been, a mother; and that even if all her children died, she would still be a mother.

A mother may not tell you about one lost. It is a secret between her and the lost one that they share in the night, or when she is alone on a dark winter afternoon. She speaks her sorrow, her grief, her if-only guilt into the winter air, and the one gone answers in a whisper.

A way to know a woman with children is to know what she holds about her children in her heart. My guess is that she will not tell you all of it. Some stories are silent in their passage from generation to generation.

My children split my bones; they fled from my body. I have cleaned them, fought with them, laughed with them, prayed for them when they were sick or in danger. They carry me along in their memories like I carry my parents and grandparents. They are the family I was and the one I will be; they are the messengers.

I stood in the doorway of the synagogue kitchen staring at the wreckage left by the bomb's blast. The ceiling had burst open and shreds of insulation and broken bits of plaster were dangling out of the gnarled gash. A metal counter had been hurled against the wall by the explosion, spilling pots and pans over the floor, smashing the bottle of wine we use for blessings. A wide stream of the wine twisted over the buckled floor, and fragments of window glass were strewn over all the surfaces in the room. The pieces still intact, hung vicious in the frame. The linoleum was riven.

It was Sunday in Boise, Idaho, 29 April 1984. Like today, as I write this, it was *Yom Ha Sho-ah*, the "Day of The Whirlwind": a time to remember and commemorate the six million Jews and five million non-Jews murdered by the Nazis in the Holocaust.

From the kitchen, I walked through the social hall to the *Bet Ha Knesset* (the sanctuary). Bewildered, I wondered, "What year is this?"—falling into the trap of linear time, as if I expected civilization to proceed by Darwinian sequence and assumed humanity was inevitably progressing toward spiritual heights of compassion, understanding, and love. I was seeing a past, a present, and a future, melded by some Kafkaesque process of time into one, and I began to shake with the depth of my own vulnerability and that of all the people I love, and I trembled in relief that the bomb had malfunctioned and exploded before the children had arrived for religious school, which is when it was meant to go off. I wondered if those who deny the Holocaust would deny this bombing and the odor of dust and destruction hanging in the air.

Later I rode home with friends.

"You know about my mother?" Benzion, a Russian Jew, asked when we stopped in front of his house.

"A pogrom?" Someone assumed.

"Yes." He sighed. "They killed her while I was sitting on her lap. I was four and the soldier was a boy of fifteen, maybe sixteen. He forced open the door and yelled, 'Give me your money, Jew.' She said, 'My husband is not home.' So, he shot her."

This week, I have been sitting at the kitchen table, spending time just looking out at the tender green of the Wasatch Front. I have been making a list of things I have read and learned.

1. There is no special prayer for this day. Every year it is a struggle beyond the use of language to communicate with each other and with G-d about this.

2. Five million of the eleven million killed were non-Jews: Gypsies, homosexuals, Poles . . . the list goes on.

3. When I look at pictures of the dead, who cannot protect their dignity or turn away from my stares, I invade their privacy and I ask forgiveness for the knowledge I must not ignore.

4. I remember and I speak of the Holocaust because I believe what Theodore Gaster teaches in his words, "Memory defies oblivion, breaks the coils of the present, establishes the continuity of the generation, and rescues human life from futility. It affords the true resurrection of the dead. The act of remembering is thus in itself redemptive."

Five mule deer wandered into
our back yard this afternoon, three yearlings and two does.
Their sloe-eyed gaze and deep coats of fur—and their grace
belie the cold. They saunter through the snow as if it were
summer and eighty degrees.

Yet, I know they are suffering. It has been below zero
for two weeks and food is scarce. The melted spot where they
lazed in the sun a month ago is covered by hard-packed snow. I
saw them nibbling twigs blown down from the tree. The
young stag has shed his antlers, those bony outgrowths of skull

that require such elaborate energy to grow and to produce velvet, only to be sloughed off every year. One fell on Tuesday and the other Saturday. Dov roved the hillside above the canal, hoping to find one because Lev was ill and Dov figured an antler would make him feel better. But the antlers had disappeared, maybe disguised as a limb of a tree, or obscured by new snow.

It is possible to see mule deer dawdling in the yards and along the sidewalks of Logan any day of the week in the winter months. Near the university, in the older development by the golf course, they idle in our yards every evening, munching on the juniper bushes or at the branches of the pine.

On a walk down the hill, by the reservoir, Steve and I saw seven. When they spotted us, they hesitated, twisting their ears like antennae. Then, the lead doe bounded in front of us, stotting across the road, to the wooded hillsides. The others followed with the same, characteristic movement, but then the littlest, like a child new to walking, veered down the middle of the pavement and headed west, the black tip of his tail bouncing against his rump.

The mule deer like this country. It is brushy on the hillsides and the Wasatch Front is patched with wooded areas. In summer the deer range on forbs and grasses, but in the winter they switch to woody plants, when they can find them. We clean out our refrigerator and rummage through our cold storage in the basement for wilted vegetables and withered apples. The first time we spread these gifts on the crusted snow, eight deer came—timid at first, but then jostling and kicking each other on the haunches with their hard black hooves. I had never seen deer fight before and I didn't like it.

Steve and I talked about hauling in hay for them, but Lev objected, "Too much fiber," he said, "they can't get the proper nutrients if they fill up on hay." He was repeating what his fourth grade teacher had told him, and we read later it was sound advice.

Some die from the cold and starvation. On a walk I found a dead doe under the bushes by Old Main. She was sitting comfortably, with her feet tucked under her chest, her body relaxed. In death, her head had simply dropped back, making a graceful arch of her neck.

Last Thursday at 3 A.M. I was shuffling down the hall to the kitchen, ready for coffee. Before I flicked on the kitchen light, I stopped at the glass doors to look out into our yard. There, in the light of the full moon, was the young stag poised in front of the bird feeder, tapping it with his nose. As he nuzzled the feeder, grain dribbled to the ground, and he bent down to feed.

One of the does that follows this stag is pregnant, and Lev and I have been calculating. If she mated in late November—a good probability—she would be two and one-half months gone, or about halfway through her pregnancy. Lev hopes he'll get to see the fawn. When I tell him it could well be twins, he grins. He imagines the herd staying the year under our elm trees, the does bearing their young in our back yard.

A few days ago I saw Lev tiptoeing across the snow toward the pine, where the stag and the pregnant doe were chewing their cuds in the sun. He moved carefully, slowly. They let him approach. I watched, intrigued, as he unzipped his jacket and slowly fanned it open. Then he carefully buried his hands in his front pants pockets and eased the pockets inside out. Finally, he circled his hands behind his backside and patted his pockets. I could see his mouth moving all the time, but through the glass doors I couldn't hear what he was saying.

When he finished and backed away, he came into the kitchen. "What were you talking to them about?" I asked him.

"Oh, I just showed them I wasn't carrying any weapons," he said. "I told them I didn't want to hurt them—so maybe the doe will have her baby here."

We are working, you see, for perfect trust.

Walking to work the other
morning, I saw five magpies on the grassy parkway eating a
thick-crust pepperoni pizza. They looked tough and low class,
like they would just as soon beat me up as look at me. From
time to time, one would hurl a piece of cheese aside, over its
wing, the way a butcher tosses a piece of fat over his shoulder
onto the floor.

My friend Norm says that from the breakfast table one
morning, he watched a mouse dart out from the basement and
scurry across the snow. When it was in the clear, Norm says,
two magpies swooped down, knocked the mouse out with

their beaks, and flew away—one of them carrying their grisly prize in its beak.

These are the facts about American magpies: They were first noted by whites on this continent on September 16, 1804, in what is now South Dakota, when they brazenly entered the tents of the men of the Lewis and Clark expedition and snatched meat out of the mens' hands. On December 1, 1806, Zebulon Pike saw magpies land on the backs of horses and peck their flesh, through oozing sores, to the bone. The horses, Pike wrote, were freezing to death, literally, and could not move. In a less macabre scenario, magpies in Manitoba have been seen to roost on the backs of cattle in a shed.

Utah magpies have relatives in Spain, Portugal, and in southeastern Siberia, among other places: the azure-winged magpie, the *cyanopica cyanus*. From these names, it seems like they should be dining in a higher class restaurant.

I stood there, in front of Frederico's, watching them. They have a way of acting like they are drunk—accidents in the air. When the wind catches their tails, they tilt and twist. On the ground, they wait for a gust of wind and then leap up to ride the current, indolent in the air as a pig in the mud. When they do fly, they fly slowly: Weary Willies loitering over the landscape mooching from the wind. So, add it up: they eat pizza for breakfast, they are indolent, they delight in dead, as well as live, meat, eggs, and baby birds.

For these things, I have wanted to dislike them. I would like to say, "Pffff! Magpies!" and move on to hummingbirds and hawks. But I can't do it. When I see a magpie's wings flash iridescent black and white, and watch it drift from the spruce down to the grass, I am awed by its beauty. And when I see them chattering together in a tree, I know their gossip is not made "tedious by morality," and I wish I could understand their stories, and could hear all the desert scuttlebutt.

I'm not the only one. Great horned, screech, and long-eared owls like magpies. Woodducks use old magpie nests (which I figure is pretty intimate); and magpies are so tight with ferruginous hawks that they have a protective nesting relationship. Magpies also get along with eagles and osprey. I mean, "Tell me who his friends are. . . ."

Lev says an old timer told him that in his day, they paid 25 cents a piece for magpie scalps.

Magpie scalps! I imagine some grizzled old mountain man hovering over a magpie carcass, his knee on its delicate breast, a bowie-knife poised above the glistening feathers of the lifeless head.

I left the magpies, still pecking at the pizza, and went on to work. That night, I sat out in our back yard in the late afternoon heat, eating chips with salsa, drinking a beer out of the bottle, and feeling very much at home in the world.

On a dark November evening,
my oldest son called me from the dojo where he studies
Tae Kwon Do.

"Quick, Mamma! Go outside. Look up at the sky.
You've got to see it!"

"Why aren't you home?" I asked him, ignoring the
urgency in his voice. He was late, and I was being a jerk.

"Mam-mah!" He wailed. "Go outside! Look up. Quick!"

It has taken me many years to learn—and still I
haven't learned it well—that when my children speak, I should

listen. They are much more observant and perceptive than I am; and Dov, the oldest, has had to suffer my stubborn character the longest.

"OK." I yielded.

I pulled my husband's heavy down coat off the hook by the door and stepped out into our driveway.

A swathe of bright shimmering red lay across the darkening sky from southeast to northwest. My son had come through with some kind of miracle—though I didn't then understand what it was I was seeing.

"Steve! Lev! Come here quick!!" I ran back inside, calling into every room.

"What, Mamma? What?" Lev bolted out of the bedroom.

"Where's Daddy?"

"Downstairs in the shower. What *is* it?" He was frustrated by my frenzy.

"Run. Get your coat, go outside and see."

I lurched down the basement stairs and banged on the bathroom door, then bounded back up again to wake my little one from his nap. Slowly, he struggled toward consciousness, twisting and stretching in a jumble with the covers. Impatient, I swiped his favorite blanket off the bed, wrapped him in it, and lugged him—still half asleep—out to the driveway.

The four of us leaned against the car, gazing up into

the sky. We made a motley crew. Lev in his jeans with no shirt or socks; Steve wrapped in a towel, steam curling off his shoulders and chest and back from the cold night air; Gidi's tender face peering out of his neon yellow bundle; me drowning in a down coat.

After a few minutes of silence, Steve grunted, "Oh, it's just smoke from some big fire." He tip-toed back toward the house, favoring his bare feet.

"No! No! Daddy." Lev called after him. "Don't go. It can't be smoke. It's too strange, too wonderful; it's got to be the northern lights."

Steve grunted again and the door closed behind him.

The red was beginning to fade. I couldn't let go; I was near tears thinking I would lose it.

"Lev, let's drive up Green Canyon."

"Can I come?" Gidi squeaked from his blanket.

"Of course!"

We clambered into the car and drove off, craning our necks for a look as we skimmed along the street toward North Logan—past the park and the field where they hold the pumpkin walk, and the stubble fields of hay—but we couldn't keep up with the turn of the earth and the flight of the heavens. By the time we reached the crossroad for Green Canyon, the light had dulled and faded, moving, it seemed, always to the west. The kids and I drove and drove, trying to catch the last glimmer. It had been our only sight ever of the *aurora bore-alis*, but even as we raced out to the mouth of the canyon, the light was gone.

I wondered, when we stopped and stepped out to search the empty sky, if that red shimmer had dissipated or if it was like clouds, moving over the earth at will, and had simply gone on north and west where other people might see it.

Those moments we were standing at the mouth of Green Canyon, I felt as lonely as I have ever felt, and I wished that we were all together. I have a fantasy about my family, a sort of dream: in it, we are a small band of hunter-gatherers, walking through the landscape. As we travel along, in our nomadic way, the movements of the world, the twists and twirls of water, air, and smoke, the etheric motions of the earth—are echoed perfectly in our hearts, as in physical fact I know they are, and we feel these motions, the inside and the outside, as one. This night, seeing the *aurora borealis* I wanted to erase the distances that existed between us: no more professor, or writer, or student, or child; no more next class or lesson, dishes, toys, or house repair; but instead some composite being holding this light in its liquid eyes—the way a deer can look—intent and curious and concentrated. I wished that when we walked away, and became our separate selves, we would carry not diverse recollections of this moment, but one single, vital memory to sustain and unite us, no matter how distant we traveled from each other.

That night, when everyone else was asleep, I left the house at 2 A.M. and drove up Logan Canyon. It still seemed to me that if I could somehow just get high enough I could catch another glimpse of that shimmering sky.

In the unnatural glare of the headlights, driving up river, I saw mule deer grazing by the roadside and a porcupine waddling to safety. Other nights this would have been enough.

Ascending toward Bear Lake, I stopped at each pullout, scanning the sky, but in the end I had to give up. The light was gone, and there was nothing for me to do but turn around and go back home.

The door of the basement
bathroom rasped open and closed, and I heard Steve calling in
a tense whisper into the family room, "Gidi. Gidi." Gidi is our
youngest son, and Steve had the voice of forced calm in the
midst of danger.

I dropped the stirring spoon into the sauce and raced
down the stairs. Steve was leaning into the doorless opening.
He had just come out of the shower and had a towel
wrapped around his waist. From above, I could see that the
muscles of his arms and back were taut. I looked in. A bat

was winging a terrified path around the room. Oblivious to it, and us, Gidi was perched on the edge of his chair mesmerized by Sesame Street.

I bent down, ran in, and scooped Gidi up in my arms. "We'll see Sesame Street in a little bit," I whispered in his ear, keeping my own adrenaline at bay, and ducking my head to stay below the flight of the bat.

Upstairs, I left Gidi in the care of one of his brothers and called to my other son to bring me the tennis racket. Taking it in hand, I bolted back downstairs. While my husband and sons waited above, I stood at the doorway and watched the frenzied circling of the bat.

In rural Iowa, in the two-story clapboard farm house where I was raised, bats in the house meant rabies. We had seen animals die of rabies. First came the odd affection: cats rubbing against dogs, skunks coming to the door, squirrels unafraid of humans, pets rolling in their own food, craving constant closeness; and then one day the sudden, vicious anger: attacks against humans, other animals, or even brooms or walls. A kitten once assailed my father and brother, biting and scratching—drawing blood—so that they were forced to put on thick winter coats and gloves and wrestle her into a gunny sack. They put the sack, which took on a frantic spirit of its own, in the back of the station wagon and drove to Iowa State University to have the kitten tested. All the way, the rough material leaped and dived, emitting screams. When they opened the bag at the lab, the kitten was foaming at the mouth.

My father and brother had to get the shots. Joe reported to me after each one: this one was in the knee, that one in the stomach, another in the back. It sounded like torture, and I thought Joe was more brave than any hero I'd ever heard of.

Now, watching this bat, I remembered our kitten, and with my own heart beating, I focused on the bat's rhythm, stepped into the open room, planted my feet, drew back, and, staring it straight in its eery face, dropped it with the only perfect overhand I have ever executed. It fell to the floor, still faintly breathing.

I leaned close over it, repulsed, and yet fascinated by its leathery skin and soft fur. Because it was small and its face looked human, it seemed like a baby itself. For that instant, I hovered above it, unsure. Then, compelled by the memory of that rabid kitten and driven by the fear for my son that still tingled in my veins, I beat the bat to death, with a force and violence it now shames me to claim.

I go to work early in the mornings; at four or five. When I walk out, no matter what season it is, the wind is blowing strong and cold from the canyon. These days it is winter, so the wind cuts at me, slicing at my waist and neck. I turn up my collar and check the sky—crystal clear and star-studded at this altitude—and walk along. I like the feel of the wind blowing my skirt in a swirl around my legs; some mornings I see mule deer in the grassy strip by the highway.

At my father's interment, when I saw the cherry wood urn that held his ashes in the hands of the undertaker, I felt a sudden rage that a stranger could touch what I so cherished. It was the way I felt when I saw the bat circling above Gidi's head.

All sense of propriety and ritual left me. I slipped my own hand out of my mother's and reached out my arms toward this man in his business suit. I had known him, this undertaker, all my life, and to me he was just a kid a few grades below me in school, and I would not let him be the one to lay my father in the earth.

My brother-in-law and I had dug my father's grave the night before at sunset. It had been one of those rare September evenings of such perfect temperature that it was impossible to distinguish the air from the skin. The sun was red and brilliant in the west, and we were on a hillside, in the spot my father had chosen, beneath two pine trees. Stopping to rest every few minutes, we had looked out over Indian Creek valley, over our own land, black satin river bottom land where the topsoil is six feet deep.

Now it was sunrise and we were burying him, and I would not let this man in the black suit, who knew nothing of the earth, hold my father.

With a startled look, he handed me the urn. I held it for a few minutes, surprised by how heavy it was, then knelt down and set it on the bottom of the grave. It was cherry wood, carved with sheaves of wheat.

I don't think I would have killed the bat if grief over my father had not been so fresh in my heart. Normally, I am more tender: when a bee gets trapped behind the curtain, I capture it in a jar and set it free in open air. I encourage the boys to let spiders be.

But for a time, rage had joined my grief and I forgot that, like the bat, I was just a thing with a human face confused by the place it had entered, trying to get my bearings, circling, circling in a tangle of light and shadow.

The doctor has decided he needs a lumbar scan of my husband's back. When I called my parents and mentioned this, my father made a funny little grunt and said, "It's really something. You ought to see it."

Waiting for the test, leaning against the hallway windows on the third floor of the hospital, we stare at the Wasatch Front. In this pure winter daylight, if it were not for the gray in his hair and beard, or the lines of pain around his eyes, Steve could be a child standing barelegged in the loose gray gown.

When the radiologist calls us from the doorway, I ask

him if I can sit in the control room. He nods and then tells Steve to lie on the smooth table that is built to move through a great white donut. Steve lies down and the radiologist shows him how to clasp his hands high above his head.

I know this man on the table. I have seen him in all moods: angry, happy, pouting and teasing, mean and sweet. I have seen him dressed and naked, have sustained him in illness and endured his snores. But I have never seen *inside* his body, the center of his bones, and now, probing into his spine, I am embarrassed, not sure I want to see this deeply: calcifications in his arteries, fatty tissues in his muscles, the armored conduit of his nerve canal, the *caude acquine*, a tangle of nerves near his tailbone. I recognize none of this as the man I know.

On the screen that shows the outer room, Steve is there, his hands clasped above his head, his face and body calm on the table. Do I want to see more?

There is no time to decide. The radiologist alerts me that I am about to see something strange, and I am too curious not to look. He has delved down to the disc space between the fifth lumbar vertebra and the first sacral vertebra.

A face appears on the screen. Millimeter by millimeter this x-ray—that surely can photograph the potential flames in a log—exposes the face of an animal: nerve roots for eyes, sacroiliac joints for ears, bodies of the first sacral nerves as cheeks, and the disc fuse, nerves wrapped around an opening, for the mouth that cannot speak.

When the machine reaches a full view of the first sacral vertebra, I meet the animal, a bear, head on. Its face is as clear as that of the one I surprised in the high salmonberry patches near Mt. Rainier. That day, I had left my friend at his lookout and started for the highway. It was sunny and warm and I was alone in the mountains, moving at my own pace through tree shadow and light, and I didn't notice when human trail turned to animal trail. Skirting a hillside, in thick second growth below a clear cut, I entered a wide salmonberry patch and was just beginning to wonder if I was lost, when a brown bear stood up—just like that—full size and puzzled in front of me. I stopped. He stared, without seeing me, I think, but he was working the air with his snout, picking up my smell, processing it. He was not angry, simply intensely alert, like me. I wanted to whistle, but my mouth was too dry. I yelled. Startled, he turned downhill and bolted over the edge of the trail, crashing through the undergrowth as he descended, barreling over bushes and flattening the seedlings in his path. I watched and listened until he was out of sight and I could no longer hear him.

At this moment, looking into Steve's bones, I feel as I did then: afraid, awed, excited by an encounter I never expected.

The radiologist tells me this face is in everyone's

bones, that we all carry a bear in the center of our backs.

I have seen this bear in the heart of my husband's marrow and now, when I look at him, his eyes are filled with visions of mountains, deer, forests, fish, pine, aspen, berries, and streams—the wilderness where I have always wanted to live.

The high, dry slopes of Cache
Valley are not like the humid flatlands of Carbondale, Illinois; and the gentle spring of 1989 did not explode like the spring of 1970. In 1970, in Carbondale, the KKK stockpiled arms to use against students at Southern Illinois University. Thousands of us, angry, saddened, and shocked by Kent State and the invasion of Cambodia, marched and yelled through the streets, making love, breaking windows, giving speeches on Main Street. The National Guard appeared in force. We were arrested, imprisoned, and tear-gassed. We fled

from the *American* army trucks that lumbered through the allies, volunteered for ACLU taking statements in the overcrowded jails, and resisted the 5 P.M. curfew.

Now in Cache Valley, I am marching again. This time, I have a son with me, and we are protesting the slaughter of whales. Ninety of us have gathered in the parking lot at Herman's Sporting Goods to begin a six-block walk to draw attention to the Icelandic whaling industry, which Iceland says is for "scientific purposes," but by which they are making $50 million a year.

We are a motley crew. The first woman I saw when I stepped out of the car was wearing bright orange eye makeup, dimestore earrings of pearls and black sequins, red silky pants, and bright plum lipstick. There were four reporters with cameras, photographing children; aging hippies; and three bigbreasted, braless freshmen with pictures of giant humpbacks undulating across their t-shirts. I counted three people wearing peace-sign jewelry. I couldn't decide if I was part of the remnant bin or if history was repeating itself.

My friend Tom said the last protest march he remembered in Logan was in 1970, that same infamous Kent State spring. "Merchants came out of their stores to shake our hands," he says, surprise flickering across his face even after nineteen years. "We thought they'd run us out of town, but they came out to shake our hands."

We spent an hour inflating multi-colored balloons, painting each one with a dark whale shape. When the march began, Tom and I walked together, trailing the younger, more eager protestors down Main Street toward the county courthouse. My son ambled behind us, talking to one of the teachers from his school.

Our route had been planned carefully. There were crossing guards at each of the lights, and a dark-haired woman jogged back and forth through the group, reminding us to walk two by two and to cross only when we were directed. We were perfectly orderly, our quiet conversations drowned by traffic.

A few million years ago, in the same place, I would have been swimming about eight miles from the northeastern shore of Lake Bonneville, the great inland sea. No whales slipped through the waters, but I like imagining the desert as a sea, like thinking of how the past glissades into present and the present slips away to the past; and today I pretend that at least one whale did scud through the waters off the Wasatch.

In reality, I am in high desert: sagebrush and bunchgrass. Near the front, the topsoil is only two inches thick and it is mule deer, not whales, ambling at the foot of the hills.

So, what do we care for whales if the only ones we ever see are plastic.

Once we reached the courthouse, Sally, a marine

biologist, sat on the steps, with her back to the wind, and talked to us about whales. She said there was reason enough to want to save whales, just because they are so big. This makes sense to me. They're just BIG. Leave them alone. Pick on somebody your own size.

After Sally, Tom speaks: "We need to find a mental space and then act . . . a mind deeper and older than the habit of destruction."

I have tried out his suggestion. Some days I sit up in the sagebrush on the front and I look out and see the ocean that was once here. The waves greet and abandon the shore, sun glints on the water at noon, gulls skim the surface of the full and vital depths. I close my eyes and imagine the ocean— because I have seen oceans and can search my memory and bring the waves to myself even on this dry shore. And I have envisioned the whales because I have seen them, so I can populate my imaginary world with them too.

This gives me little peace. It is my sons I care about now. I want them to learn grace from a live orca in the water, to learn patience from the owl, to see a condor owning the air, and so, know what it is to fly.

Last week Kim came for a visit. After breakfast we drove up river for a walk at Guinavah-Malibu. It was a perfect morning: golden and cold, and the boys clamored to sit next to Kim on the way up.

When we turned off the highway into the trees and got out of the car, we all calmed down. Maybe it was the shadows of the bare cottonwood, the darkening. We walked toward the river, talking in quiet tones.

The river means much to all of us: summer afternoons I take the boys to a spot under the wooden bridge where the water is shoulder high. We dare each other to jump in with no prelude. I am often the first: I close my eyes, fall into the icy flow, and come up sputtering, gasping, laughing. Finally, the boys go in—they can stay longer than I; they seem impervious to the cold. Relishing the afternoon heat and sun, I watch them from a rock on the bank.

I go to the river too, if I have something important to tell my sons. When my father was dying I took them there often; it is the place I can tell them about many of the things he told me. I show them the pygmy owl, the eagle, the muskrat. We have seen rattlesnakes, trout, moose, deer, and porcupine. What my father taught me was sacred, I can show them at the river.

And I go to the river alone when it is necessary to understand some event in my life that I cannot understand among people. I look there for an end to illness or for an answer to a disagreement. The clear intensity of the muskrat perched on the edge of the ice feeding, or of the rattlesnake sliding through the rocks and heat of a dry summer, gives me a perspective I like to keep, something to hold onto in a world that keeps sliding out of whack.

We walked along. In a depression under a giant cottonwood, we spotted a doe, sitting, with her neck in a gentle arch. The kids fell back, quiet.

"Something's wrong." Kim spoke.

"Yes, she should be startled. She should bound off." I agreed with him.

We approached slowly. She watched without moving, though there was fear in her eyes.

When we got within a rod of her, she began to flounder, pawing at the earth, struggling to rise. Her hindquarters were shattered.

We drove back down canyon and called the highway patrol. They promised they would go right up.

The next day the boys and I were watching a low blanket of clouds move along the base of the front, south toward the canyon. At the mouth of the canyon, the fog suddenly stood up and began to climb heavenward. We were seeing the architecture of the wind. One of the boys said, "Maybe it's a spirit rising, showing itself on the way." We looked at each other and ran to get our coats.

The night had changed the trail at Guinavah. Branches had fallen in the wind; there was a light covering of snow. I looked for signs as we walked. Had we come this way yesterday?

Yes. There she was, looking at me, her ears alert, her gaze direct—either from pain or from numbness. She retained her dignity even in dying; she watched.

I felt angry. The highway patrol hadn't acted. They carry guns and *can* kill it and haven't.

We drive back down river. The wife of the conservation officer says, "Well, he'll do something if I can get ahold of him."

I give her directions: "If he just follows my tracks—the snow is fresh—and stops where they stop, he'll see her, straight in front of him."

I cannot act and I cannot not act. She is in pain, dying of thirst and starvation. Or she is dying of internal injuries. How long has she been there? None of this is right.

On the third day, she was gone. The boys and I drove up through the bright morning sunshine. Walking toward the place, we saw a long trail of deer droppings and I knew that someone had shot her and carried her out.

There were no other signs: no human tracks, no tread marks; the leaves were undisturbed; there was no blood where she had lain; no trace of final struggle.

My middle son said, "Maybe they came and fixed her and already she's up in the hills running through the forest." His eyes trailed over the rimrock as if he could see her there. "Be happier now, Mamma."

My oldest son grunted, "They didn't *fix* her, Lev; it would cost the state too much money and besides, they couldn't fix her so fast."

Each insisted.

On the way back to the car, I saw an empty box of

Remington 22 longs—a green and yellow box untouched by snow and the wet.

My middle son looked at the box, then at me. Taking my arm, he says, "Next winter, Mamma, we'll see her bounding through the snow."

Someone told us that three
years ago there were no beavers on the creek where we like to
walk. Walking there early last spring, we counted sixteen dams
in under a mile.

I am obsessed with this phenomenon, and go back to
the creek often to walk up stream, counting the dams, assuring
myself that environmentally all is not disaster and destruction—that there is growth, health.

By late spring I had counted the dams many times,
but had yet to see a beaver. So, one chilly morning, my son,

Lev, and I set the alarm for 3:30 A.M. and by four were lying on a groundsheet on a rise over a bend in the creek where it broadens into a marsh. We shivered and waited. At first light, Lev noticed movement to our right. It was a beaver, trolling through the water—his nose breaking the way, his tail swaying in the wake.

We watched; he stopped to inspect branches, then swam on upstream toward the large dam above us, his nose and eyes and ears alert, intent on progress. We watched until he was out of sight in the overgrowth.

Now, winter again, the water level is low. I go back anyway—sometimes with the kids and sometimes alone. The river, the creeks flowing into it, the beaver—it is the balance for me: a sanity and health I offer myself and the kids. I need to escape not only from the town and highways, but even from our house, where, daily, the radio broadcasts violence, corruption, and cruelty.

Last Saturday we went up river to count the dams again. Part way to our favorite spot, I noticed a moose feeding on brush on the far side of the creek. We stood still and watched her. She was alert, but calm. From time to time she turned to check on us, but continued to feed.

Snowmobilers zoomed out from around a corner, skidded to avoid hitting us, and roared away. The moose stopped feeding to watch this fiasco, then turned back to the brush. Cross-country skiers glided by, intent on their stride.

"Moose," I said to one of them.

He stopped, took off his goggles and looked at me as if I had made a pass at him. "What? What did you say?"

"Moose," I said and pointed, laughing. How could anyone, out skiing on a beautiful morning with a moose across the river, in one of the most enchanting canyons in the world, be grumpy?

"I didn't think they came down this low," his companion quipped as she adjusted her goggles.

They strode away, slapping the gentle snow with their skis, absorbed by health.

We went back the next day, to see if she was still there. She was. Lying in the snow, just a few feet from where she had been feeding. At first sight, I thought she was a shadow; I had to strain my eyes to see her true form. Lev decided he would shuttle across a fallen log to the other side of the creek to get a better look. She watched him. He climbed a tree on the far side. They watched each other. When Lev came back, he said, "I think I'll climb the hill. That way I can look down on her and get a clear view. It's the way hunters do it."

He started up through the snow. Gidi, my little one, trailed after him.

I think Lev was right about the hunters, because as soon as he started up the slope, the moose rose, alert.

I followed their progress: Lev's blue jacket ascending through the snow, Gidi's labored zigzag to tread in his older brother's steps. About thirty yards up, Lev turned and sank into the snow, leaning against the hill. Below him, Gidi did the same. The moose watched from across the creek.

It started to snow. I could feel myself enveloped in the swirl of snowflakes. As I disappeared in the whiteout, I looked out and saw my sons and the moose joined by curiosity and awe, staring at each other across the water. In this moment of perfect peace, I stood dead still and let the snow take me.